# At the Zoo

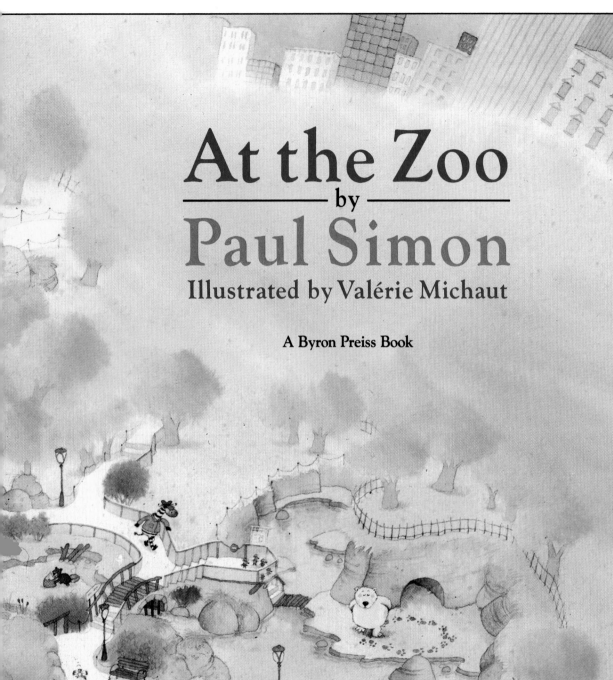

# At the Zoo
## by
# Paul Simon
## Illustrated by Valérie Michaut

A Byron Preiss Book

Doubleday

New York   London   Toronto   Sydney   Auckland

Someone told me
it's all happening
at the zoo.
I do believe it,
I do believe it's true.

It's a light and tumble journey
from the East Side to the park.

Just a fine and fancy ramble to the zoo.

But you can take the crosstown bus
if it's raining or it's cold.

And the animals will love it if you do.

Something tells me
it's all happening
at the zoo.
I do believe it,
I do believe it's true.

The monkeys stand for honesty.

GIRAFFE

POLAR BEAR

POLAR BEAR

Giraffes are insincere.

And the elephants are kindly but they're dumb.

**Orangutans are skeptical
of changes in their cages.**

**And the zookeeper is very fond of Rum.**

Zebras are reactionaries.

Antelopes are missionaries.

Pigeons plot in secrecy...

. . . and hamsters turn on frequently.

**What a gas!**

# You gotta come
and see at the zoo!

PUBLISHED BY DOUBLEDAY
a division of Bantam Doubleday Dell Publishing Group, Inc.
666 Fifth Avenue, New York, New York 10103

DOUBLEDAY and the portrayal of an anchor
with a dolphin are trademarks of Doubleday,
a division of Bantam Doubleday Dell Publishing Group, Inc.

Special thanks to Stephen Rubin, Shaye Areheart,
Jacqueline Onassis, Peter Kruzan,
Stephen and Nathalie Brenninkmeyer,
Marino Degano, and the Central Park Zoo.

Editor: Gillian Bucky

Library of Congress Cataloging-in-Publication Data

Simon, Paul, 1941–
At the zoo / Paul Simon; illustrated by Valérie Michaut.—1st ed.
p. cm.
Summary: A light and tumble journey across town to the zoo can
bring encounters with the honest monkeys, kindly elephants, and skeptical orangutans.

1. Children's songs—Texts. [1. Zoo animals—Songs and music.
2. Songs.] I. Michaut, Valérie, ill. II. Title.
PZ8.3.S594At 1991
782.42164'0268—dc20          91-4351
                                CIP
                                AC

ISBN 0-385-41771-3
ISBN 0-385-41906-6 (lib. bdg.)